DISCUSSION PAPER 65

I0102182

LAND RIGHTS AND CITIZENSHIP IN AFRICA

CHRISTIAN LUND

NORDISKA AFRIKAINSTITUTET, UPPSALA 2011

Indexing terms:
Africa
Land reform
Land tenure
Property rights
Citizenship
Social research

Language checking: Peter Colenbrander

ISSN 1104-8417

ISBN 978-91-7106-705-0

© The author and Nordiska Afrikainstitutet 2011

Production: Byrå4

Print on demand, Lightning Source UK Ltd.

Contents

Foreword

This Discussion Paper explores the close relationship between land rights and citizenship in Africa. It also provides a broad overview of the state of existing knowledge on land rights and citizenship and its implications for development in Africa. In this regard, it provides deep insights into the literature on the subject and explores the conceptual approaches to problems related to land rights in Africa. It is noted by the author that the land issue in Africa is not a monolithic phenomenon requiring a single remedy, but is a bundle of issues spanning access to and control over natural resources; distribution of power among the state, citizens, and local systems of authority; and everyday struggles over land involving claims, counter-claims and the struggles for survival. The paper provides a good discussion of the concepts and debates around land rights and citizenship. It analyses citizenship in terms of the relationship between citizens and public authority; social, political and property rights as they relate to notions of autochthony; and 'layered' identities. The discussion includes the issue of gendered citizenship and discrimination against women in terms of access to land and the conditions under which they may hold it without being considered the owners of land or able to engage in land transactions on the same level as men. The paper also provides an analysis of the formalisation of land tenure/rights, competing formalisations, informalisation and the challenges posed by growing population size, rapid urbanisation, tourism, conservation, commercialisation, privatisation of land, including land grabbing by big foreign agro-business investing in commercial food or biofuel production. Some of the consequences of this trend, such as land enclosures, new forms of identity and mobility, the attendant exclusion of certain groups from accessing land on the basis of their identities or competing land use, and the dynamics that drive social tensions and conflict in the face of increased commodification (and scarcity) of land are explored. This provides a context for raising critical conceptual and research questions and identifying areas of policy engagement by scholars working on the subject in terms of the connections between land rights and citizenship in Africa, exploring the space for land reform in the face of competing and conflicting demands and uses, and mapping the positive and negative processes of security, exclusion and vulnerability as they emerge on the continent. In this regard, this paper provides a very rich resource for scholars as well as research groups and academic institutions seeking to take some of the issues relating to the land rights/citizenship struggles in Africa forward.

Cyril Obi
Senior Researcher
The Nordic Africa Institute

Introduction

Land rights and land reform have reappeared on the development agenda in the Global South over the past 15 years. However, no uniform identification of the problem, of the approach and of the instruments exists. As Wolford[1] succinctly puts it, mainstream development institutions, governments and social movements often have different readings of past reform efforts and of prescriptions for the future. Mainstream development institutions such as the World Bank argue that land reform requires *getting prices right*. This entails removal of government interventions or policies that create market distortions and imperfections (see de Janvry et al. 2001; World Bank 2003). Supporters of government-led reform often contend that land rights and land reform are about *getting policies right*. Their thinking reflects the concern with establishing rules and regulations for ownership, transactions, expropriation and redistribution (Binswanger-Mkhize et al. 2009; Bruce and Migot Adholla 1994; Fitzpatrick 2005, 2006; Platteau 1996; Toulmin and Quan 2000; Toulmin, Lavigne Delville and Traoré 2002; Ubink, Hoekema and Assies 2009). Finally, an emerging group of actors – more present in Latin America and Asia than in Africa – consisting of movements and activists, argue that land rights and successful land reform hinges on *getting the politics right*. According to this group, the political will of government to go against the interests of the powerful and wealthy classes is crucial for any policy to succeed (Amanor 2002; Moyo and Yeros 2002). While such reform efforts may be analytically distinct, they are often pursued in conjunction with each other, in combination and sometimes in contradiction of each other.

When dealing with the land issue in Africa it is therefore advisable to keep a few basics in mind. First, there is no single land issue. A whole series of issues are, among other things, expressed in terms of access to and control over natural resources, that is, in terms of land tenure. Slow growth, limited technological innovation, equity, social security and conflict are all concerns that somehow relate to land. Not all are equally pressing in all circumstances and their respective priorities are essentially political. Land policies express, implicitly or explicitly, the political choices made about the distribution of power among the state, its citizens and local systems of authority.

From this follows the second basic observation: There is no single remedy or instrument to deal with land issues. Had there been a magic bullet, it almost certainly would have been fired by now. Frustration with the complexity of land-related problems may render decision-makers susceptible to 'clear-cut,' 'once-and-for-all,' seemingly 'obvious solutions.' But simplistic policies have a

---

1. For the division into three groups of reform proponents of reform, I am indebted to Wendy Wolford's talk at the LUCE Conference, Berkeley, 2 June 2010.

truly poor record in Africa. However, inaction and refusal to deal with land issues politically is not a real option. 'Autonomous' land dynamics have significant socioeconomic and political effects, not all of which are benign. There is no 'natural evolution' of land tenure systems: they are integral parts of social and political processes (Bruce 1986; Colin and Woodhouse 2010; Platteau 1996).

This takes us to the third basic observation. Land issues are in fact not new in Africa. The land tenure situation has always been undergoing change in response to demographic and technological changes, wars, conquests and changes in governance. Moreover, land has been an object of policy intervention from colonial times to the present, and every spot of land in Africa has a history of changing land policies and different forms of land politics. Any new policy and related research must therefore take previous policies and their effects into account.

The purpose of this paper is to provide a broad overview, and examine the issues of land rights and citizenship and their ramifications for African development. The concept of land used in this context generally refers to agricultural land, pasture, forests, water and other natural resources. The paper undertakes a broad overview of the literature and proposes a conceptual approach to the discussion of a number of problems related to questions of land rights in Africa. In particular, issues of the formalisation of rights, redistribution of rights, land enclosures and mobility will be discussed in relation to a broad definition of citizenship.

The paper also identifies and discusses some areas for further research and policy-relevant engagement by scholars working in the area of land rights and citizenship in Africa.

Although the scope of the paper is vast, its length is modest, but it does point to the critical issues and areas in the research topic. In places, the paper draws on the work by Lund, Odgaard and Sjaastad (2006).

Land Rights and Citizenship – Concepts and Features of the Debate

Few things are more fundamental in social life or politics than what we have and who we are. Property and social identity, in the broadest sense, are perhaps the most overt and familiar manifestations of these core dimensions. Few issues in Africa connect the two aspects more intimately than land, where claims to land are partly defined by social identity, and social identity partly defined through property (see Lund 2006; Sikor and Lund 2010). The two concepts need some elaboration.

Land Rights

Land is important for the livelihoods of the majority of African populations and the social and economic development of society. Growing pressure on land resources, land-related conflicts and rural impoverishment make land rights a crucial political issue.

Land rights, or property, is about relationships among social actors with regard to objects of value. Property relations involve different kinds of social actors, including individuals and collectivities and take the form of 'enforceable claim[s] to some use or benefit of something' (MacPherson 1978: 3). Property relations exist at the level of laws and regulations, cultural norms and social values, actual social relationships and property practices. Property is a claim sanctioned by some form of public authority. Struggles over property are, therefore, as much about the scope and constitution of authority as about access to resources. How people acquire and secure land rights might seem a straightforward question. However, it soon gets complicated when we realise that more often than not several competing normative orders may be brought to bear to legitimise a specific claim, and several groups and institutions may compete over the jurisdiction to settle disputes and set norms by precedent.

Increasingly, the argument of belonging has been brought to bear both as a claim to resources and to jurisdictions. Obviously, this also produces a broad array of processes in which people may engage in order to pursue their interests. These range from a 'low-tension'-level, where people aim to pre-empt competing claims by performing and establishing legitimising symbols, to open disputes and conflicts handled by formal state-mandated or supervised courts – or indeed enacted outside them. In this sense, the issue of land is not, as such, particular, but one among a range of issues over which political and legal struggles intertwine, where local powers and less localised power structures interact and where political and cultural symbols of power and authority are brought into play. We often talk about such conflicts as 'land conflicts' but, as indicated, there is always more at stake. It is never merely a question of land but a question of property, and social and political relationships in a very broad sense.

Property relations in postcolonial and specifically African settings are often ambiguous because of the multiplicity of institutions competing to sanction and validate (competing) claims in attempts to gain authority for themselves. Social actors struggle over the very categories and relationships constituting property (Sikor and Lund 2010). The large body of literature analysing the dynamics of property from recent decades includes Basset and Crummey (1993), Berry (1985, 1993, 2001, 2002a+b); Chanock (1985); Colin and Woodhouse (2010); Comaroff and Roberts (1981); Derman, Odgaard and Sjaastad (2007); Downs and Reyna (1988); Evers, Spirenburg and Wels (2005); Juul and Lund (2002); Le Roy, Karsenty and Bertrand (1995); Lund (2008); Moore (1978, 1986); Peters (1994); Shipton (1989, 2009); Shipton and Goheen (1992); Toulmin, Lavigne Delville and Traoré (2002); and Toulmin and Quan (2000). The relationship between people and specific political institutions invokes the concept of citizenship.

Citizenship

Citizenship, according to Bellamy (2008: 3), refers to 'a particular set of political practices involving specific public rights and duties with respect to a given political community.' The focus is on the relationship of rights and obligations between members of this community. Citizenship is generally – though not always – organised as a relationship between individuals and an institution of public authority, but it does not exclusively refer to national citizenship – this is just one of several configurations. It is basically shorthand for people's political subjectivity and agency. It denotes through which political institution a person derives rights of membership to that community. In Africa, land is a resource to which access is ensured not merely by membership of a national community – local citizenship and status are often as or more important.

Jacob and Le Meur (2010) discuss and develop the concept of citizenship in relation to property in Africa. They observe that just as multiple sets of rules prevail, and pluralities of institutions compete to exercise authority over the allocation of rights in most African societies, so is belonging layered. While people have a national citizenship, which endows them with certain rights, it is not the only significant form of belonging in a political community and the only source of rights. A first distinction that seems to be invoked increasingly in African and other societies is what we could term national and local citizenship. While people may share national citizenship, the idea of autochthony – first arrival – is often invoked as a mechanism of inclusion and exclusion (Bayart et al. 2001; Berry 2010; Chauveau 2006; Geschiere 2010). Citizenship – or political membership – implies rights to have rights, so to speak. Some of the most conspicuous recent conflicts over land where belonging – or autochthony – has been instrumentalised have played out in Côte d'Ivoire (Chauveau 2006) and Cameroon (Geschiere 2010), but it would appear to be an almost generic feature of land rights in Africa. In some areas, however, such as Southern Nigeria, local communities have failed dismally when trying to exclude government and/or foreign commercial interests from what they consider to be their areas (Watts 1997, 2003, 2004). In essence, it is a question of how interventionist a central government is in overseeing rights and how much is left for the local level to sort out, and whether instrumentalisation of different forms of citizenship takes place nationally and/or locally (Boone 2003; Lentz 1998, 2006a). Much research documents how a narrowing definition of belonging is one of the key dynamics in the differentiation of land rights and access to resources (Peters 2009). Deliberate simplification of a complex composite tenure system can be instrumentalised for exclusionary purposes.

In the broad sense, one can view citizenship as being layered according to more than seniority in a place. However, gender is another distinction that runs like a deep structure through most systems of land rights. While national citizenship rarely – if at all – formally discriminates between men and women, local citizenships are often segmented to the detriment of women. In some societies, women are considered 'legal minors' whose land may be their possession but not their property: woman landholders are considered to hold the land in trust for their sons, and cannot engage in transactions on the same footing as men (see Bryceson 1995; Diarra and Monimart 2004, 2006; Monimart and Diarra 2009; Griffiths 1997; Hellum et al. 2007; Sitko 2010; Whitehead and Tsikata 2003).

It is not that social identity, membership and status automatically entail rights, but they can make it legitimate to claim them. Conversely, not belonging, not being a local citizen, may deny the person a legitimate opportunity to stake a claim. The categories of citizens – or those entitled to seek entitlements – are not carved in stone. Groups can slide out of certain categories while others enter it and entrench themselves. Hahonou's research in Niger is an illuminating example (2006, 2008, 2009, 2010, 2011). Appointments of locals to different public positions have systematically favoured the nobles, and servile status is in principle incompatible with exercise of political office. In some places, a local organisation managed to mobilise and organise city people – businessmen and active and retired civil servants – of servile origin who represented the larger electorate. At the end of the day, descendants of slaves won a majority of seats and the mayor was chosen from their midst, and it became more difficult to overrule property claims by this group in tenure commissions, etc.

In sum, citizenship and land rights are closely connected in most African societies. Citizenship and belonging can be avenues to secure property, and property may bolster claims of belonging and citizenship. Both elements – rights and political identity – are dynamically malleable. This dynamic is not straightforward, however. It configures differently depending on the context and the issue at stake. The following sections will briefly sketch out some of the issues and coin a number of research issues.

Formalisation of Rights

The colonial state, whether British, French, Portuguese, Belgian or German, at an early stage introduced legislation to regulate, formalise and register the use of and access to resources in Africa. Such initiatives ranged from expropriation and eviction of local people through various forms of nationalisation and exclusion, systems of permits and concessions, the introduction of taxes to delegation of control to local chiefs and other authorities who acted as custodians of the amorphous entity known as the 'natives.' Often such 'native citizenship' was hardened into categories of tribes and groups with specific rights and status (Berry 1993; Bruce 1986; Chanock 1985; Mamdani 1996; Mann and Roberts 1991; McAusland 2000; Moore 1986). Today, formalisation of land and water rights in Africa continues under various labels: decentralisation, *gestion de terroir*, community-based natural resource management, user pays principle, land or water reform, tenure reform and privatisation (Sikor and Müller 2008).

Official formalisation is, however, often paralleled by other forms of competing formalisations of rights. The considerable flexibility of indigenous land tenure arrangements in Africa is widely documented (Berry 2002; Juul and Lund 2002; Toulmin, Lavigne Delville and Traoré 2002; Benjaminsen and Lund 2003; Evers et al. 2005). Recent experience shows that growing population pressure and development of markets in connection with commercialisation of agriculture have given rise to significant changes in land tenure practices, namely in terms of the dynamics of privatisation and formalisation.

Autonomous processes of privatisation, of exclusion and of outright land grabbing are often accompanied by different efforts at addressing land rights (Lavigne Delville 1998, 2003; Mathieu, Zongo and Paré 2003). As a consequence of the unsatisfied demand for formalisation of land rights, a process of what one might call 'informal' formalisation is emerging in many places with land scarcity. Thus, informal recording of property transactions on paper, or other formalised ways of registration and transaction, seem to develop in parallel with states' generally less than successful efforts at formally recording the land tenure situation (Lavigne-Delville 2003). Such informal practices are produced and invented through local institutional innovation, using whatever means available.

Most African societies experience a commodification of land. While this often entails some formalisation, access to land may become commoditised without extinguishing the socio-political dimension of land transactions (Chauveau and Colin 2010). Thus, markets may well be segmented, reserved for some while inaccessible to others, provide guarantees for some while constituting risk for others, etc. One of the fundamental conflicts seems to be whether land is alienable or not, and indeed what status – citizenship – does it require to transact in different markets?

Along with commodification of land, ownership often narrows down. In larger communities, common property is often carved up and individualised, benefiting certain segments capable of invoking privileges derived from their status (as autochthones, as nobility, as men, etc.). In families, common ownership is often transformed into one man's ownership.

These developments provoke the following questions that need to be researched further:

- How are official and unofficial forms of formalisation of land rights articulated?
- How and to what extent does status and local citizenship facilitate or preclude the pursuit of and securitisation of property rights?
- How and to what extent does status and local citizenship facilitate or preclude participation in the land market?
- How do different forms of status and citizenship change over time?
- How are different forms of status and citizenship instrumentalised by political forces?

Redistribution of Land

Redistribution programmes are responses to historically skewed distributions of land. In Africa, this is mainly a legacy of the colonial period. Attention to land redistribution has been strongest of late in Kenya, Malawi, Namibia, South Africa and Zimbabwe. Motivations for the redistribution of land extend beyond the obvious need to address issues of equality and social justice to include objectives related to production and efficiency (Binswanger-Mkhize et at. 2009). While it would appear that there is a growing consensus about the rationale for redistributive land reform, the results are mixed.

Most redistributive land reform efforts have a socioeconomic perspective and are putatively 'blind' to questions of citizenship. In South Africa, for example, intense debates about the possible role of customary leaders in the allocation and administration of communal land have informed policy (Cousins and Claasens 2008. See also Ubink and Amanor 2008 for parallel issues in Ghana). And in cases of redistribution and group title, the dynamics of the group are interesting and not fully researched. Whether membership of such ownership groups depends on (or develops) cultural affiliation, and how such affiliation serves to protect, include and exclude different people and essentially serve to build up privileges, remains an open question and concern for further research.

The following research questions are relevant:

- How and to what extent does status and local citizenship facilitate or preclude access to benefits from land redistribution?
- How is legal personality provided to customary and other groups?
- How does land distribution – especially to groups – influence the creation and reproduction of local citizenship?

Land Enclosures

The phenomenon of land enclosures in Africa has recently become more acute. If we use the term enclosure loosely, it means legally or physically (sometimes violently) fencing off a particular area, usually by government or large organisations (donors or companies), excluding past uses and users, in order to commit the area to new land use. There are several configurations of this process. One is the establishment of forest or wildlife reserves, excluding people from what used to be 'their' resources (Basset and Crummey 2003; Tilley 2003). This has often affected distinct groups (e.g., the Barabaig and the Maasai in Tanzania), which have experienced a status as second-class citizens whose claims and rights have been virtually ignored by government. This has continued in various forms, such as conservation, and recently so-called REDD (Reducing Emissions from Deforestation and Forest Degradation) projects, where agreements are made between government and donors and local populations.

Recently, large-scale land concessions for food or biofuel production have been granted by governments to domestic and foreign operators. This is sometimes referred to as land grabbing. Foreign investors buy, lease or in other ways acquire concessions to large tracts of land (Cotula et al. 2009; FAO 2009; Horta 2009). The interest of the company is to access cheap land and produce food or fuel. The interest of the government is to receive investment for economic development. For the local population, opportunities for work may materialise.

However, 'many countries do not have in place legal or procedural mechanisms to protect local rights and take account of local interests, livelihoods and welfare' (Cotula et al. 2009: 7). Especially where this implies contract farming of commercial crops by local residents in exchange for rights to stay on what they believed was their land, questions of property and citizenship reconfigure. With whom do small-scale 'share-croppers' engage in a property rights relationship, and how do rights of citizenship develop between government institutions, donors, landholding companies, and local residents and incoming – sometimes foreign – migrant workers?

Research has been conducted on conservation and exclusion (Adams and Humle 2001; Hulme and Murphree 2001; Wily and Haule 1995) and research on the impact of REDD and other 'participatory' conservation schemes is emerging (Ezra 2010). However, the local consequences of large-scale land acquisition in Africa have not yet been thoroughly investigated.

The following research questions are relevant:

- Who are effectively whose tenants in the new configuration of government, concessionary companies and smallholders?
- How do land concessions affect local land rights and what status groups are the most vulnerable?

Mobility

There are two fundamental and general issues in relation to migration and mobility and land rights. One is the aspect of being first-comers or latecomers in certain areas, or indigenous versus non-indigenous/newcomers. While this may not cause a big problem as long as land is plentiful, there is much evidence that it certainly does cause problems as competition for land increases. Such problems often form along ethnic lines (Juul and Lund 2002; Toulmin 2006; Odgaard 2003 and 2005; Peters 1994). War and other forms of unrest also set people in motion, sometimes crossing international borders. This obviously invokes questions of citizenship and land rights.

The other basic issue is the type of land use. In terms of claiming land it makes a big difference whether land is cultivated, and thus appears with visible signs of use, or whether it is being used as pastures, or for hunting and gathering activities, for example, by more or less mobile groups of people. For the latter livelihood patterns it has been shown how difficult it is for the groups practising them to claim any land rights at all, even in their original home areas (IIED 1999; Juul 2005; Lane and Pretty 1990; Loftsdóttir 2008; Tenga 1992; Odgaard 2005). While this challenge has been the major reason behind the migration of such people to other parts of their countries or abroad in the first place, migration certainly makes it even more difficult for them to claim land in the areas to which they move.

The land tenure systems evolving in areas with heavy immigration are extremely complex. Immigration produces a complicated mix of local indigenous rules and norms, informal renting and borrowing arrangements, semi-formal agreements (in writing) and formally registered rights, all of which often coexist and even overlap. Often, migrants in a particular place originate from the same region and benefit from contacts and connections established by their predecessors (Breusers 1998; Chauveau 2006; Kuba et al. 2003).

In the many fast-growing cities in Africa with the increasing numbers of squatters and growing slum areas, the situation in relation to tenure and tenancy rights and access to other resources is often chaotic. Not surprisingly, such areas are often very conflict-ridden.

The following are important research questions:

- How do groups of migrants acquire land rights in their place of arrival?
- What is the nature and duration of such rights?
- Are 'new' rights differentiated according to status (ethnicity, gender, age, etc.)?
- Do land rights lead to other forms of political participation?

A Processual Perspective

Engaging with the nexus of land rights and citizenship requires a processual perspective. The connection between land rights and citizenship is dynamic. Not only do land rights evolve in a political process, so do different forms of belonging and status. In a certain way, women, migrants, commoners, youth and others who may be disenfranchised at certain moments, may 'graduate' to full or fuller citizenship. Conversely, rights can erode when certain forms of identity are stigmatised, devalued or otherwise marginalised. In general, it is politically essential, and academically challenging, to identify and understand the recursive reproduction of rights and identity. And there is a significant task in mapping out positive and negative processes of security and exclusion and patterns of vulnerability.

References

Adams, W. and D. Hulme, 2001, 'Conservation and Community,' in D. Hulme and M. Murphree (eds), *African Wildlife and Livelihoods*. Oxford, James Currey. pp. 9–23.

Amanor, K., 1999, *Global Restructuring and Land Rights in Ghana. Forest Food Chains, Timber and Rural Livelihoods*. Uppsala, Nordic Africa Institute.

—, 2002, 'Night harvesters, forest hoods and saboteurs. Struggles over land expropriation in Ghana,' in S. Moyo and P. Yeros (eds), *Reclaiming the Land. The Resurgence of Rural Movements in Africa, Asia and Latin America*. London, Zed Books. pp. 102–17.

—, 2010, 'Family values, land sales and agricultural commodification in southeastern Ghana.' *Africa* vol. 80, no. 1, pp. 104–25.

Atwood, D.A., 1990, 'Land registration in Africa: The impact on agricultural production.' *World Development* vol. 18, no. 5, pp. 659–71.

Ault, G. and D. Rutman, 1979, The development of individual rights to property in tribal Africa.' *Journal of Law and Economics* vol. 22, no. 1, pp. 163–82.

Basset, T.J. and D.E. Crummey (eds), 1993, *Land in African Agrarian Systems*. Madison, University of Wisconsin Press.

Basset, T.J. and D.E. Crummey (eds), 2003, *African Savannas. Global Narratives and Local Knowledge of Environmental Change*. Oxford, James Currey.

Bates, R., 1983, *Essays on the Political Economy of Rural Africa*. Berkeley, University of California Press.

Bayart, J.-F., 1989, *L'État en Afrique. La politique du ventre*. Paris, Fayard.

Bayart, J.-F., P. Geschiere and F. Nyamnjoh, 2001, 'Autochtonie, démocratie et citoyenneté en Afrique.' *Critique Internationale* no. 10, pp. 177–94.

Bellamy, R., 2008, *Citizenship. A Very Short Introduction*. Oxford, Oxford University Press.

Benjaminsen, T.A. and C. Lund, 2002, 'Formalisation and informalisation of land and water rights in Africa.' *European Journal of Development Research* vol. 14, no. 2, pp. 1–10.

Berry, S., 1985, *Fathers Work for their Sons – Accumulation, Mobility and Class Formation in an Extended Yorùbá Community*. Berkeley, University of California Press.

—, 1988, 'Concentration without privatization? Some consequences of changing patterns of rural land control in Africa,' in R.E. Downs and S.P. Reyna (eds), *Land and Society in Contemporary Africa*. Hanover/London, University Press of New England. pp. 53–75.

—, 1989, 'Social institutions and access to resources.' *Africa* vol. 59, no. 1, pp. 41–55.

—, 1992, 'Hegemony on a shoestring – indirect rule and access to agricultural land.' *Africa* vol. 62, no. 3, pp. 327–55.

—, 1993, *No Condition is Permanent – the Social Dynamics of Agrarian Change in sub-Saharan Africa*. Madison, University of Wisconsin Press.

—, 1997, 'Tomatoes, land and hearsay. Property and history in Asante in the time of structural adjustment.' *World Development* vol. 25, no. 8, pp. 1225–41.

—, 2001, *Chiefs Know their Boundaries. Essays on Property, Power, and the Past in Asante, 1896–1996*. Portsmouth/Oxford, Heinemann/James Currey.

—, 2002a, 'The everyday politics of rent-seeking. Land allocation on the outskirts of Kumase, Ghana,' in K. Juul. and C. Lund (eds), *Negotiating Property in Africa*. Portsmouth. Heinemann.

—, 2002b, 'Debating the Land Questions.' *Comparative Studies in Society and History* vol. 44, no. 4, pp. 638–68.

— 2010, 'Property, authority, and citizenship. Land claims, politics and the dynamics of social division in West Africa,' in T. Sikor and C. Lund (eds), *Politics of Possession*. London, Blackwell. pp. 23–45.

Bierschenk, T., J.-P. Chauveau and J.-P. Olivier de Sardan, 2000, 'Les courtiers entre développement et État,' in T. Bierschenk, J.-P. Chauveau and J.-P. Olivier de Sardan (eds), *Courtiers en développement. Les villages africains en quête de projets*. Paris, Karthala. pp. 5–42.

Bierschenk, T. and J.-P. Olivier de Sardan, 1997, 'Local powers and a distant state in rural Central African Republic.' *Journal of Modern African Studies* vol. 35, no. 3, pp. 441–68.

—, 1998, 'Les arènes locales face à la décentralisation et à la démocratisation,' in T. Bierschenk and J.-P. Olivier de Sardan (eds), *Les pouvoirs au village. Le Bénin rural entre démocratisation et décentralisation*. Paris, Karthala. pp. 11–51.

—, 2003, 'Powers in the village. Rural Benin between democratisation and decentralisation.' *Africa* vol. 73, no. 2, pp. 145–73.

Binswanger-Mkhize, H.P., C. Bourguignon and R. van den Brink (eds), 2009, *Agricultural Land Distribution. Toward Greater Consensus*. Washington DC, World Bank.

Bohannan, P., 1963, '"Land", "tenure" and land-tenure,' in D. Biebuyck (ed.), *African Agrarian Systems*. Oxford, Oxford University Press. pp. 101–15.

Boone, C., 1998, 'State building in the African countryside: Structure and politics at the grassroots.' *Journal of Development Studies* vol. 34, no. 4, pp. 1–31.

—, 2003, *Political Topographies of the African State. Territorial Authority and Institutional Choice*. Cambridge, Cambridge University Press.

Breusers, M., 1998, *On the Move. Mobility, Land Use and Livelihood Practices on the Central Plateau in Burkina Faso*. Wageningen, Wageningen Agricultural University.

Bruce, J. and S.E. Migot-Adholla (eds), 1994, *Searching for Land Tenure Security in Africa*. Dubuque, Kendall/Hunt Publishers.

Bruce, J., 1993, 'Do indigenous tenure systems constrain agricultural development?' in T.J. Basset and D.E. Crummey (eds), *Land in African Agrarian Systems*. Madison, University of Wisconsin Press. pp. 35–56.

Bruce, J., S. Migot-Adholla and J. Atherton, 1994, 'Institutional adaptation or replacement,' in J Bruce and S.E. Migot-Adholla (eds), *Searching for Land Tenure Security in Africa*. Dubuque, Kendall/Hunt Publishers. pp. 251–66.

Bryceson, D.F. (ed.), 1995, *Women Wielding the Hoe*. Oxford, Berg Publishers.

Chanock, M., 1991a, 'A peculiar sharpness – an essay on property in the history of customary law in colonial Africa.' *Journal of African History* vol. 32, no.1, pp. 65–88.

—, 1991b, 'Paradigms, policies and property. A review of the customary law of land tenure,' in K. Mann and R. Roberts (eds), *Law in Colonial Africa*. Portsmouth, Heinemann. pp. 61–84.

—, 1998, *Law, Custom and Social Order. The Colonial Experience in Malawi and Zambia*. Portsmouth, Heinemann.

Chauveau, J.-P., 2000, 'Question foncière et construction nationale en Côte d'Ivoire.' *Politique Africaine* no. 78, pp. 94–125.

Chauveau, J.-P., 2006, 'Les transferts coutumiers de droits entre autochtones et "étrangers,"' in J.-P. Chauveau, J.-Ph. Colin, J.-P. Jacob, Ph. Lavigne Delville and P.-Y. Le Meur (eds), *Modes d'accès à la terre, marchés fonciers, gouvernance et politiques foncières en Afrique de l'Ouest*. London, CLAIMS/IIED. pp. 16–29.

—, 2007, *La loi de 1998 sur les droits fonciers coutumiers dans l'histoire des politiques foncières en Côte d'Ivoire*. Working Paper. Montpellier, IRD/INRA

Chauveau, J.-P. and P. Mathieu, 1998, 'Dynamiques et enjeux des conflits fonciers,' in Ph. Lavigne-Delville (ed.), *Quelles politiques foncières pour l'Afrique rurale? Réconcilier pratiques, légitimité et légalité*. Paris, Karthala. pp. 243–58.

Chauveau, J.-P. and J.-P. Colin, 2010, 'Customary transfers and land sales in Côte d'Ivoire. Revisiting the embeddedness issue.' *Africa* vol. 80, no. 1, pp. 81–103.

Chimhowu, A., and P. Woodhouse, 2010, 'Forbidden but not suppressed. A "vernacular" land market in Svosve communal lands, Zimbabwe.' *Africa* vol. 80, no. 1, pp. 14–35.

Claasens, A. and B. Cousins (eds), *Land, Power and Custom*. Athens OH, Ohio University Press.

Colin, J.-P. and P. Woodhouse, 'Introduction: interpreting land markets in Africa.' *Africa* vol. 80, no. 1, 2010, pp. 1–13.

Comaroff, J. L. and S. Roberts, 1981, *Rules and Processes – the Cultural Logic of Dispute in an African Context*. University of Chicago Press, Chicago.

Cotula, L., S. Vermeulen, R. Leonard and J. Keeley, 2009, *Land Grab or Development Opportunity? Agricultural Investment and International Land Deals in Africa*. London, IIED.

Cousins, B., 1997, 'How do Rights become Real?' *IDS Bulletin* 28, no. 4, October, pp. 59–68.

—, 2002, 'Legislating negotiability. Tenure reform in post-apartheid South Africa,' in K. Juul and C. Lund (eds), *Negotiating Property in Africa*. Portsmouth, Heinemann. pp. 67–101.

de Janvry, A., G. Gordillo, J.-P. Platteau and E. Sadoulet (eds), 2001, *Access to Land, Rural Poverty and Public Action*. Oxford, Oxford University Press.

de Soto, H., 2000, *The mystery of capital: Why capitalism triumphs in the West and fails everywhere else*. New York, Basic Books.

Demsetz, H., 1967, 'Toward a theory of property rights.' *American Economic Review* vol. 57, no. 2, pp. 347–59.

Derman, B., R. Odgaard and E. Sjaasatd (eds), 2007, *Conflicts over Land and Water in Africa*. Oxford, James Currey.

Diarra, M. and M. Monimart, 2006, 'Landless women, hopeless women? Gender, land and decentralisation in Niger.' *IIED Issue Paper* no. 143.

Doka, M. and M. Monimart, 2004, 'Women's access to land. The de-feminisation of agriculture in rural Niger?' *IIED Issue Paper* no. 128.

Downs, R.E. and P. Reyna (eds), 1988, *Land and Society in Contemporary Africa*. Hanover NH, University Press of New England.

Evers, S., M. Spierenburg and H. Wels (eds), 2005, *Competing Jurisdictions. Settling Land Claims in Africa*. Leiden, Brill.

Ezram Z., 2010, 'The new way of bio-colonialism.' *Anuyak Media* 26 January.

Fairhead, J. and M. Leach, 1998, *Reframing deforestation. Global analysis and local realities: studies in West Africa*. London and New York, Routledge.

FAO, 2009, Land acquisitions in Africa pose risk for poor. Available on: http://www.fao.org/news/story/en/item/19974/icode/

Firmin-Sellers, K., 1996, *The Transformation of Property Rights in the Gold Coast*. Cambridge, Cambridge University Press.

—, 2000, 'Custom, capitalism, and the state. The origins of insecure land tenure in West Africa.' *Journal of Theoretical and Institutional Economics* vol. 156, pp. 513–30.

Fisiy, C., 1992, *Power and Privilege in the Administration of Law – Land Law Reform and Social Differentiation in Cameroon*. PhD Dissertation, Leiden, African Studies Centre.

Fitzpatrick, D., 2005, '"Best Practice" options for the legal recognition of customary tenure.' *Development and Change* vol. 36, no. 3, pp. 449–75.

—, 2006, 'Evolution and chaos in property rights systems. The Third World tragedy of contested access.' *Yale Law Journal* vol. 115, no. 5, pp. 996–1048.

Fortmann, L., 1995, 'Talking claims. Discursive strategies in contesting property.' *World Development* vol. 23, no. 6, pp. 1053–63.

Geschiere, P., 2009, *The Perils of Belonging. Autochthony, Citizenship, and Exclusion in Africa and Europe*. Chicago, University of Chicago Press.

Geschiere, P. and J. Gugler, 1998, 'The urban-rural connection, Changing issues of belonging and identification.' *Africa*, vol 68. no. 3, pp. 309–17.

Griffiths, A., 1997, *In the Shadow of Marriage. Gender and Justice in an African Community*. Chicago, Chicago University Press.

Hahonou, E., 2006, *En attendant la décentralisation au Niger ... Dynamiques locales, clientélisme et culture politique*. PhD Dissertation, EHESS, Marseille.

—, 2008, 'Culture politique, ésclavage er décentralization. La revanche politique des descendants d'esclaves au Bénin et au Niger.' *Politique Africaine* no. 111, pp. 169–86.

—, 2009, 'Slavery and politics: Stigma, decentralisation, and political representation in Niger and Benin,' in B. Rossi (ed.), *Reconfiguring Slavery: West African Trajectories*. Liverpool, Liverpool University Press. pp. 152–81.

—, 2010, *Démocratie et culture politique en Afrique. En attendant la décentralisation au Niger*. Editions Universitaires Européennes, Sarrebruck.

—, forthcoming 2011, 'Past and present citizenships of slave descent: Lessons from Benin.' *Citizenship Studies* vol. 15, no. 1.

Hailey, W.M. (Lord), 1938, *An African Survey. A Study of Problems Arising in Africa South of the Sahara*. Oxford, Oxford University Press.

Hellum, A., J. Stewart, S. Shaheen Ali and A. Tsanga (eds), 2007, *Human Rights, Plural Legalities and Gendered Realities*. Harare, Weaver Press.

Horta, L., 2009, Food security in Africa. China's new rice bowl. Available on: http://farmlandgrab.org/3053

IIED, 1999, *Land Tenure and Resource Access in West Africa: Issues and Opportunities for the Next Twenty-Five Years*. London, International Institute for the Environment and Development.

Jacob, J.-P. and P.-Y. Le Meur, 2010, 'Citoyenneté locale, foncier, appartenance et reconnaissance dans les sociétés du Sud,' in J.-P. Jacob and P.-Y. Le Meur (eds), *Politique de la terre et de l'appartenance. Droits fonciers et citoyenneté locale dans les sociétés du Sud*. Paris, Karthala. pp. 5–57.

Juul, K., 2005, *Tubes, Tenure and Turbulence, The Effects of Drought Related Migration on Tenure Systems and Resource Management in Northern Senegal*. Hamburg, LIT Verlag.

Juul, K. and C. Lund (eds), 2002, *Negotiating Property in Africa*. Portsmouth, Heinemann.

Kuba, R., C. Lentz and C. Nurukyor Somda (eds), 2003, *Histoire du peuplement et relations interethniques au Burkina Faso*. Paris, Karthala.

Kuba, R. and C. Lentz (eds), 2006, *Land Rights and the Politics of Belonging in West Africa*. Leiden, Brill.

Lane, C. and J. N. Pretty, 1990, *Displaced Pastoralists and Transferred Wheat Technology in Tanzania,'* IIED Gatekeeper Series no. SA20.

Lavigne Delville, P., 1998, *Quelles Politiques Foncières Pour L'Afrique Rurale? Réconcilier Pratiques, Légitimité et Légalité*. Paris, Karthala/Coopération Francaise.

—, 1999, 'Mieux connaître les pratiques paysannes d'usage de l'écrit dans les transactions foncières, enjeux scientifiques et opérationnels,' in Ph. Lavigne-Delville and P. Mathieu (eds), *Formalisation des contrats et des transactions. Repérage des pratiques populaires d'usage de l'écrit dans les transactions foncières en Afrique rurale.* Paris/Louvain-la-Neuve, GRET/Institut des Etudes du Développement, Université Catholique de Louvain. pp. 4–12.

Le Meur, P.-Y., 2002, 'Trajectories for the politicisation of land issues. Case studies from Benin,' in K. Juul and C. Lund (eds), *Negotiating Property in Africa.* Portsmouth, Heinemann. pp. 135–56.

Le Roy, É., 1984, 'Legal paradigm and legal discourse – the case of laws of French-speaking Black Africa.' *International Journal of the Sociology of Law* no. 12, pp. 1–22.

—, 1985, 'La loi sur le domaine national a vingt ans: joyeux anniversaire?' *Monde en Développement* vol. 13, no. 52, pp. 667–85.

—, 1991a, 'L'État, la réforme et le monopole foncier,' in le Bris, É., É. Le Roy and P. Mathieu (eds), *L'appropriation de la terre en Afrique noire*, Paris : Karthala Editions.

—, 1991b, 'Les usages politiques du droit,' in C. Coulon and D.-C. Martin (eds.), *Les Afriques politiques.* Paris, Éditions la Découverte. pp. 109–22.

Le Roy, É., A. Karsenty and A. Bertrand, 1995, *La sécurisation foncière en Afrique. Pour une gestion viable des ressources renouvellables.* Paris, Karthala.

Leach, M., R. Mearns and I. Scoones, 1997, *Environmental Entitlements – A Framework for Understanding the Institutional Dynamics of Environmental Change.* Brighton, IDS Discussion Paper no. 359.

Lentz, C. and P. Nugent (eds), 2000, *Ethnicity in Ghana. The Limits of Invention.* London, Macmillan. pp. 1–28.

Lentz, C., 1998, *Die Konstruktion von Ethnizität. Eine Politische Geschichte Nord-West Ghanas, 1870–1990.* Köln, Köppe Verlag.

—, 2006a, *Ethnicity and the Making of History in Northern Ghana.* Edinburgh, Edinburgh University Press.

—, 2006b, 'Decentralization, the state and conflicts over local boundaries in Northern Ghana.' *Development and Change* vol. 37, no. 4, pp. 901–19.

—, 2006c, 'Land rights and the politics of belonging in Africa,' in R. Kuba and C. Lentz (eds), *Land Rights and the Politics of Belonging in West Africa.* Leiden, Brill. pp. 1–34.

Loftsdóttir, K., 2008, *The Bush is Sweet. Identity, Power and Development among WoDaaBe Fulani in Niger.* Uppsala, Nordic Africa Institute.

Lund, C., 1998, *Law, Power and Politics in Niger – Land Struggles and the Rural Code*. Hamburg, LIT Verlag.

—, 2002, 'Negotiating property institutions. On the symbiosis of property and authority in Africa,' in K. Juul and C. Lund (eds), *Negotiating Property in Africa*. Portsmouth, Heinemann. pp. 11–44.

—, 2006, 'Twilight institutions. Public authority and local politics in Africa.' *Development and Change* vol. 37, no. 4, pp. 685–705.

—, 2008, *Local Politics and the Dynamics of Property in Africa*. Cambridge, Cambridge University Press.

Lund, C., R. Odgaard and E. Sjaastad, 2006, *Land Rights and Land Conflicts in Africa. A Review of Issues and Experiences*. Report commissioned by the Danish Ministry of Foreign Affairs, Denmark. http://www.diis.dk/graphics/Publications/Andet2007/rod_landrights_SOA.doc.pdf'

MacPherson, C.B., 1978, *Property – Mainstream and Critical Positions*. Oxford, Blackwell.

Mann, K. and R. Roberts, 1991, 'Law in colonial Africa,' in K. Mann and R. Roberts (eds), *Law in Colonial Africa*. Portsmouth/London, Heinemann/James Currey. pp.3–58.

Mathieu, P., M. Zongo and L. Paré, 2002, 'Monetary land transactions in Western Burkina Faso. Commoditisation, papers and ambiguities.' *European Journal of Development Research* vol. 14, no. 2, pp. 109–28.

McAusland, P., 2000, 'Only the name of the country changes. The diaspora of "European" land law in Commonwealth Africa,' in C. Toulmin and J. Quan (eds), *Evolving Land Rights, Policy and Tenure in Africa*. London, IIED/Natural Resources Institute. pp. 75–95.

Migot-Adholla, S. and J. Bruce, 1994, 'Are indigenous African tenure systems insecure?' in J. W. Bruce and S.E. Migot-Adholla (eds), *Searching for Land Tenure Security in Africa*. Dubuque, Kendall/Hunt. pp. 1–14.

Migot-Adholla, S., P.B. Hazell, B. Blarel and F. Place, 1993, 'Indigenous land rights systems in Sub-Saharan Africa, A constraint on productivity?' in K. Hoff, A. Braverman and J. Stiglitz (eds), *The Economics of Rural Organization*. Oxford, Oxford University; Press/World Bank. pp. 269–91.

Monimart, M. and M. Diarra, 2009, *Enjeux de genre: Foncier et regeneration naturelle assistée. Elements de reflexion collectés dans six communautés de la region de Maradi*. Copenhagen, Care.

Moore, S.F., 1978, *Law as Process*. London, Routledge and Kegan Paul.

—, 1986, *Social Facts and Fabrications – 'Customary' Law on Kilimanjaro 1880–1980*. Cambridge, Cambridge University Press.

—, 1998, 'Changing African land tenure. Reflections on the incapacities of the state.' *European Journal of Development Research* vol. 10, no. 2, pp. 33–49.

Mortimore, M., 1999, 'History and evolution of land tenure and administration in West Africa.' IIED Issue Paper no. 71. London, International Institute for Environment and Development.

Moyo, S. and P. Yeros (eds), 2005, *Reclaiming the Land. The Resurgence of Rural Movements in Africa, Asia and Latin America*. London, Zed Books.

Odgaard, R., 2005, 'The struggle for land rights in the context of multiple normative orders in Tanzania,' in S. Evers, M. Spierenburg and H. Wels (eds), *Competing Jurisdictions: Settling Land Claims in Africa*. Leiden, Brill.

Ouedraogo, R.S., J.-P. Sawadogo, V. Stamm and T. Thombiano, 1996, 'Tenure, agricultural practices and land productivity in Burkina Faso. Some recent results.' *Land Use Policy* vol. 13, no. 3, pp. 229–32.

Paré, L., 1999, 'Les pratiques de formalisation des transactions foncières dans l'ouest burkinabé,' in Ph. Lavigne-Delville and P. Mathieu (eds), *Formalisation des contrats et des transactions. Repérage des pratiques populaires d'usage de l'écrit dans les transactions foncières en Afrique rurale*. Paris/Louvain-la-Neuve, GRET/Institut des Etudes du Développement, Université Catholique de Louvain. pp. 89–94.

Peters, P., 1994, *Dividing the Commons. Politics, Policy and Culture in Botswana*. Charlottesville/London, University Press of Virginia.

—, 2002, 'The limits of negotiability: Security, equity and class formation in Africa's land systems,' in K. Juul and C. Lund (eds), *Negotiating Property in Africa*. Portsmouth, Heinemann.

—, 2004, 'Inequality and social conflict over land in Africa.' *Journal of Agrarian Change* vol. 4, no. 3, pp. 269–314.

—, 2009, 'Challenges in land tenure and land reform in Africa. Anthropological perspectives.' *World Development* vol. 37, no 8, pp. 1317–25.

Place, F., 2009, 'Land tenure and agricultural productivity in Africa. A comparative analysis of the economics literature and recent policy strategies and reforms.' *World Development* vol. 37, no. 8, pp. 1326–36.

Platteau J.-P., 1996, 'The Evolutionary Theory of Land Rights as Applied to Sub-Saharan Africa, A Critical Assessment.' *Development and Change* vol. 27, no. 1, pp. 29–86.

Prag, E., 2004, *Women Making Politics. Women's Associations, Female Politicians and Development Brokers in Rural Senegal.* PhD Dissertation, Roskilde University.

Ribot, J. and N. Peluso, 2003, 'A Theory of Access.' *Rural Sociology* vol. 68, issue 2.

Ribot, J., 1995, 'From exclusion to participation. Turning Senegal's forestry policy around?' *World Development* vol. 23, no. 9, pp. 1587–99.

Rose, C., 1994, *Property and Persuasion – Essays on the History, Theory and Rhetoric of Ownership.* Boulder CO, Westview Press.

Schlager, E. and E. Ostrom, 1992, 'Property rights regimes and natural resources – a conceptual analysis.' *Land Economics* no. 3, pp. 249–62.

Shipton, P. and M. Goheen, 1992, 'Understanding African land-holding, Power, wealth and meaning.' *Africa* vol. 63, no. 3, pp. 307–25.

Shipton, P., 1988, 'The Kenyan land reform, Misunderstandings in the public creation of private property,' in R.E. Downs and S.P. Reyna (eds), *Land and Society in Contemporary Africa.* Hanover NH, University of New England Press. pp. 91–134.

—, 1989, *How Private Property Emerges in Africa – Directed and Undirected Land Tenure Reforms in Densely Settled Areas South of the Sahara.* Boston, Harvard University (HIID and Dept. of Anthropology).

—, 2009, *Mortgaging the Ancestors.* New Haven, Yale University Press.

Sikor, T. and C. Lund (eds), 2010, *Politics of Possession. Property, Authority, and Access to Natural Resources.* London, Blackwell.

Sikor, T., and D. Müller, 2009, 'The limits of state-led reform.' *World Development* vol. 37, no. 8, pp. 1307–16.

Sitko, N., 2010, 'Fractured governance and local frictions. The exclusionary nature of clandestine land markets in southern Zambia.' *Afric,* vol. 80, no. 1, pp. 36–55.

Sjaastad, E. and D.W. Bromley, 1997, 'Indigenous land rights in Sub-Saharan Africa, Appropriation, security and investment dynamics.' *World Development* vol. 25, no. 4, pp. 549–62.

Stamm, V. and J.-P. Sawadogo, 1995, *Structures foncières et gestion des terroirs au Burkina Faso.* Ouagadougou, CEDRES.

Tenga, R., 1992, *Pastoral Land Rights in Tanzania, A Review.* IIED Drylands Programme: Pastoral Land Tenure Series.

Tilley, H., 2003, 'African Environments and Environmental Sciences,' in W. Beinart, and J. McGregor (eds), *Social History and African Environments*. Oxford, James Currey. pp. 109–130.

Toulmin, C. and J. Quan, 2000, *Evolving Land Rights, Policy and Tenure in Africa*. London, IIED/Natural Resources Institute.

Toulmin, C., P. Lavigne Delville and S. Traoré (eds), 2002, *The Dynamics of Resource Tenure in West Africa*. Oxford, James Currey.

Ubink, J. and K. Amanor (eds), 2008, *Contesting Land and Custom in Ghana. State, Chief and the Citizen*. Leiden, Leiden University Press.

Ubink, J., A.J. Hoekema and W.J. Assies (eds), 2009, *Legalising Land Rights. Local Practices, State Responses and Tenure Security in Africa, Asia and Latin America*. Leiden, Leiden University Press.

van Rouveroy van Nieuwaal, E.A.B., 1999, 'Chieftaincy in Africa: Three facets of a hybrid role,' in E.A.B van Rouveroy van Nieuwaal and R. van Dijk (eds), *African Chieftaincy in a New Socio-Political Landscape*. Hamburg, LIT Verlag. pp. 21–48.

Watts, M., 1997, 'Black Gold, White Heat: State Violence, Local Resistance and the National Question in Nigeria,' in S. Pile and M. Keith (eds), *Geographies of Resistance*. New York and London, Routledge.

—, 2003, 'Economies of Violence: Governable and Ungovernable Spaces in an Oil Nation [Nigeria].' Paper delivered to the Comparative Politics Workshop, University of Chicago, 18 November.

—, 2004, 'Resource curse? Governmentality, oil and power in the Niger Delta, Nigeria.' *Geopolitics* vol. 9, no. 1, pp. 50–80.

Whitehead, A., and D. Tsikata, 2003, 'Policy discources on women's land rights in Sub-Saharan Africa. The implications of the return to the customary.' *Journal of Agrarian Change* vol. 3, nos 1–2, pp. 67–112.

Wiley, L. and O. Hauke, 1995, "Good News from Tanzania: The first village forest reserves in the making – the story of Duro-Haitemba". FAO Forests, Trees and People Newsletter. vol. 29. pp. 28–38.

World Bank, 1974, *Land Reform*. Washington DC, World Bank.

—, 2003, *Land Policies for Growth and Poverty Reduction*. Washington DC, World Bank.

Zongo, M., 1999, 'Transactions foncières et usage de l'écrit dans la zone co-
tonière du Burkina Faso,' in Ph. Lavigne-Delville and P. Mathieu (eds), *Formalisation des contrats et des transactions. Repérage des pratiques populaires
d'usage de l'écrit dans les transactions foncières en Afrique rurale.* Paris/Lou-
vain-la-Neuve, GRET/Institut des Etudes du Développement, Université
Catholique de Louvain. pp. 77–87.

DISCUSSION PAPERS PUBLISHED BY THE INSTITUTE

Recent issues in the series are available electronically for download free of charge
www.nai.uu.se

1. Kenneth Hermele and Bertil Odén, *Sanctions and Dilemmas. Some Implications of Economic Sanctions against South Africa.* 1988. 43 pp. ISBN 91-7106-286-6

2. Elling Njål Tjønneland, *Pax Pretoriana. The Fall of Apartheid and the Politics of Regional Destabilisation.* 1989. 31 pp. ISBN 91-7106-292-0

3. Hans Gustafsson, Bertil Odén and Andreas Tegen, *South African Minerals. An Analysis of Western Dependence.* 1990. 47 pp. ISBN 91-7106-307-2

4. Bertil Egerö, *South African Bantustans. From Dumping Grounds to Battlefronts.* 1991. 46 pp. ISBN 91-7106-315-3

5. Carlos Lopes, *Enough is Enough! For an Alternative Diagnosis of the African Crisis* 1994. 38 pp. ISBN 91-7106-347-1

6. Annika Dahlberg, *Contesting Views and Changing Paradigms.* 1994. 59 pp. ISBN 91-7106-357-9

7. Bertil Odén, *Southern African Futures. Critical Factors for Regional Development in Southern Africa.* 1996. 35 pp. ISBN 91-7106-392-7

8. Colin Leys and Mahmood Mamdani, *Crisis and Reconstruction – African Perspectives.* 1997. 26 pp. ISBN 91-7106-417-6

9. Gudrun Dahl, *Responsibility and Partnership in Swedish Aid Discourse.* 2001. 30 pp. ISBN 91-7106-473-7

10. Henning Melber and Christopher Saunders, *Transition in Southern Africa – Comparative Aspects.* 2001. 28 pp. ISBN 91-7106-480-X

11. *Regionalism and Regional Integration in Africa.* 2001. 74 pp. ISBN 91-7106-484-2

12. Souleymane Bachir Diagne, et al., *Identity and Beyond: Rethinking Africanity.* 2001. 33 pp. ISBN 91-7106-487-7

13. Georges Nzongola-Ntalaja, et al., *Africa in the New Millennium.* Edited by Raymond Suttner. 2001. 53 pp. ISBN 91-7106-488-5

14. *Zimbabwe's Presidential Elections 2002.* Edited by Henning Melber. 2002. 88 pp. ISBN 91-7106-490-7

15. Birgit Brock-Utne, *Language, Education and Democracy in Africa.* 2002. 47 pp. ISBN 91-7106-491-5

16. Henning Melber et al., *The New Partnership for Africa's development (NEPAD).* 2002. 36 pp. ISBN 91-7106-492-3

17. Juma Okuku, *Ethnicity, State Power and the Democratisation Process in Uganda.* 2002. 42 pp. ISBN 91-7106-493-1

18. Yul Derek Davids, et al., *Measuring Democracy and Human Rights in Southern Africa.* Compiled by Henning Melber. 2002. 50 pp. ISBN 91-7106-497-4

19. Michael Neocosmos, Raymond Suttner and Ian Taylor, *Political Cultures in Democratic South Africa.* Compiled by Henning Melber. 2002. 52 pp. ISBN 91-7106-498-2

20. Martin Legassick, *Armed Struggle and Democracy. The Case of South Africa.* 2002. 53 pp. ISBN 91-7106-504-0

21. Reinhart Kössler, Henning Melber and Per Strand, *Development from Below. A Namibian Case Study.* 2003. 32 pp. ISBN 91-7106-507-5

22. Fred Hendricks, *Fault-Lines in South African Democracy. Continuing Crises of Inequality and Injustice.* 2003. 32 pp. ISBN 91-7106-508-3

23. Kenneth Good, *Bushmen and Diamonds. (Un) Civil Society in Botswana.* 2003. 39 pp. ISBN 91-7106-520-2

24. Robert Kappel, Andreas Mehler, Henning Melber and Anders Danielson, *Structural Stability in an African Context.* 2003. 55 pp. ISBN 91-7106-521-0

25. Patrick Bond, *South Africa and Global Apartheid. Continental and International Policies and Politics.* 2004. 45 pp. ISBN 91-7106-523-7

26. Bonnie Campbell (ed.), *Regulating Mining in Africa. For whose benefit?* 2004. 89 pp. ISBN 91-7106-527-X

27. Suzanne Dansereau and Mario Zamponi, *Zimbabwe – The Political Economy of Decline.* Compiled by Henning Melber. 2005. 43 pp. ISBN 91-7106-541-5

28. Lars Buur and Helene Maria Kyed, *State Recogni-tion of Traditional Authority in Mozambique. The nexus of Community Representation and State Assist-ance.* 2005. 30 pp. ISBN 91-7106-547-4

29. Hans Eriksson and Björn Hagströmer, *Chad – Towards Democratisation or Petro-Dictatorship?* 2005. 82 pp.ISBN 91-7106-549-

30. Mai Palmberg and Ranka Primorac (eds), *Skinning the Skunk – Facing Zimbabwean Futures.* 2005. 40 pp. ISBN 91-7106-552-0

31. Michael Brüntrup, Henning Melber and Ian Taylor, *Africa, Regional Cooperation and the World Market – Socio-Economic Strategies in Times of Global Trade Regimes.* Com-piled by Henning Melber. 2006. 70 pp. ISBN 91-7106-559-8

32. Fibian Kavulani Lukalo, *Extended Handshake or Wrestling Match? – Youth and Urban Culture Celebrating Politics in Kenya.* 2006.58 pp. ISBN 91-7106-567-9

33. Tekeste Negash, *Education in Ethiopia: From Crisis to the Brink of Collapse.* 2006. 55 pp. ISBN 91-7106-576-8

34. Fredrik Söderbaum and Ian Taylor (eds) *Micro-Regionalism in West Africa. Evidence from Two Case Studies.* 2006. 32 pp. ISBN 91-7106-584-9

35. Henning Melber (ed.), *On Africa – Scholars and African Studies.* 2006. 68 pp. ISBN 978-91-7106-585-8

36. Amadu Sesay, *Does One Size Fit All? The Sierra Leone Truth and Reconciliation Commission Revisited.* 2007. 56 pp. ISBN 978-91-7106-586-5

37. Karolina Hulterström, Amin Y. Kamete and Henning Melber, *Political Opposition in African Countries – The Case of Kenya, Namibia, Zambia and Zimbabwe.* 2007. 86 pp. ISBN 978-7106-587-2

38. Henning Melber (ed.), *Governance and State Delivery in Southern Africa. Examples from Botswana, Namibia and Zimbabwe.* 2007. 65 pp. ISBN 978-91-7106-587-2

39. Cyril Obi (ed.), *Perspectives on Côte d'Ivoire: Between Political Breakdown and Post-Conflict Peace.* 2007. 66 pp. ISBN 978-91-7106-606-6

40. Anna Chitando, *Imagining a Peaceful Society. A Vision of Children's Literature in a Post-Conflict Zimbabwe.* 2008. 26 pp. ISBN 978-91-7106-623-7

41. Olawale Ismail, *The Dynamics of Post-Conflict Reconstruction and Peace Building in West Africa. Between Change and Stability.* 2009.52 pp. ISBN 978-91-7106-637-4

42. Ron Sandrey and Hannah Edinger, *Examining the South Africa–China Agricultural Relationship.* 2009. 58 pp. ISBN 978-91-7106-643-5

43. Xuan Gao, *The Proliferation of Anti-Dumping and Poor Governance in Emerging Economies.* 2009. 41 pp. ISBN 978-91-7106-644-2

44. Lawal Mohammed Marafa, *Africa's Business and Development Relationship with China. Seeking Moral and Capital Values of the Last Economic Frontier.* 2009. xx pp. ISBN 978-91-7106-645-9

45. Mwangi wa Githinji, *Is That a Dragon or an Elephant on Your Ladder? The Potential Impact of China and India on Export Led Growth in African Countries.* 2009. 40 pp. ISBN 978-91-7106-646-6

46. Jo-Ansie van Wyk, *Cadres, Capitalists, Elites and Coalitions. The ANC, Business and Development in South Africa.* 2009. 61 pp. ISBN 978-91-7106-656-5

47. Elias Courson, *Movement for the Emancipation of the Niger Delta (MEND). Political Marginalization, Repression and Petro-Insurgency in the Niger Delta.* 2009. 30 pp. ISBN 978-91-7106-657-2

48. Babatunde Ahonsi, *Gender Violence and HIV/AIDS in Post-Conflict West Africa. Issues and Responses.* 2010. 38 pp. ISBN 978-91-7106-665-7

49. Usman Tar and Abba Gana Shettima, *Endangered Democracy? The Struggle over Secularism and its Implications for Politics and Democracy in Nigeria.* 2010. 21 pp. ISBN 978-91-7106-666-4

50. Garth Andrew Myers, *Seven Themes in African Urban Dynamics.* 2010. 28 pp. ISBN 978-91-7106-677-0

51. Abdoumaliq Simone, *The Social Infrastructures of City Life in Contemporary Africa.* 2010. 33 pp. ISBN 978-91-7106-678-7

52. Li Anshan, *Chinese Medical Cooperation in Africa. With Special Emphasis on the Medical Teams and Anti-Malaria Campaign.* 2011. 24 pp. ISBN 978-91-7106-683-1

53. Folashade Hunsu, *Zangbeto: Navigating the Spaces Between Oral art, Communal Security And Conflict Mediation in Badagry, Nigeria.* 2011. 27 pp. ISBN 978-91-7106-688-6

54. Jeremiah O. Arowosegbe, *Reflections on the Challenge of Reconstructing Post-Conflict States in West Africa: Insights from Claude Ake's Political Writings.*
    2011. 40 pp. ISBN 978-91-7106-689-3

55. Bertil Odén, *The Africa Policies of Nordic Countries and the Erosion of the Nordic Aid Model: A comparative study.*
    2011. 66 pp. ISBN 978-91-7106-691-6

56. Angela Meyer, *Peace and Security Cooperation in Central Africa: Developments, Challenges and Prospects.*
    2011. 47 pp ISBN 978-91-7106-693-0

57. Godwin R. Murunga, *Spontaneous or Premeditated? Post-Election Violence in Kenya.*
    2011. 58 pp. ISBN 978-91-7106-694-7

58. David Sebudubudu & Patrick Molutsi, *The Elite as a Critical Factor in National Development: The Case of Botswana.*
    2011. 48 pp. ISBN 978-91-7106-695-4

59. Sabelo J. Ndlovu-Gatsheni, *The Zimbabwean Nation-State Project. A Historical Diagnosis of Identity and Power-Based Conflicts in a Postcolonial State.*
    2011. 97 pp. ISBN 978-91-7106-696-1

60. Jide Okeke, *Why Humanitarian Aid in Darfur is not a Practice of the 'Responsibility to Protect'.*
    2011. 45 pp. ISBN 978-91-7106-697-8

61. Florence Odora Adong, *Recovery and Development Politics. Options for Sustainable Peacebuilding in Northern Uganda.*
    2011, 72 pp. ISBN 978-91-7106-698-5

62. Osita A. Agbu, *Ethnicity and Democratisation in Africa. Challenges for Politics and Development.*
    2011, 30 pp. ISBN 978-91-7106-699-2

63. Cheryl Hendricks, *Gender and Security in Africa. An Overview.*
    2011, 32 pp. ISBN 978-91-7106-700-5

64. Adebayo O. Olukoshi, *Democratic Governance and Accountability in Africa. In Search of a Workable Framework.*
    2011, 25 pp. ISBN 978-91-7106-701-2

65. Christian Lund, *Land Rights and Citizenship in Africa.*
    2011, 31 pp. ISBN 978-91-7106-705-0